THE ALLIGATOR'S SMILE
AND OTHER POEMS

JANE YOLEN
PHOTOGRAPHS BY JASON STEMPLE

MILLBROOK PRESS • MINNEAPOLIS

For young David Stemple, teeth and tail, his kind of book —J.Y.

For Caroline and Amelia, who love all alligators,
big and small —J.S.

Millbrook Press
A division of Lerner Publishing Group, Inc.
241 First Avenue North
Minneapolis, MN 55401 USA

For reading levels and more information, look up this title at www.lernerbooks.com.

Acknowledgments: "Seven Words about an Alligator" © 2014, published in *Poetry Friday Science Anthology*, Wong and Vardell.

Additional images: © Irina Bg/Shutterstock.com (reptile skin background); © Johan Knelsen/Shutterstock.com (reeds).

Design by Emily Harris
Main body set in Avenir Next 17/38. Typeface provided by Linotype AG.

Library of Congress Cataloging-in-Publication Data

Names: Yolen, Jane, author. | Stemple, Jason, photographer.
Title: The alligator's smile and other poems / written by Jane Yolen ; photographs by Jason Stemple.
Description: Minneapolis : Millbrook Press, [2017]
Identifiers: LCCN 2015044329 (print) | LCCN 2015044383 (ebook) | ISBN 9781467755757 (lb : alk. paper) |
    ISBN 9781512411102 (eb pdf)
Subjects: LCSH: Alligators—Juvenile poetry.
Classification: LCC PS3575.O43 A6 2017 (print) | LCC PS3575.O43 (ebook) | DDC 811/.54—dc23

LC record available at http://lccn.loc.gov/2015044329

Manufactured in the United States of America
1-36802-17694-2/25/2016

Contents

Seven Words about an Alligator . . . 5

The Alligator's Smile . . . 6

Alligator to Himself . . . 8

Mother and Child, Alligator Style . . . 10

Kindergarten for Alligators . . . 12

Sunning . . . 14

Alligator in Armor . . . 16

So Many Teeth . . . 18

Mother Alligator on the Path . . . 20

Ambush . . . 22

What an Alligator Eats . . . 24

Obituary . . . 26

Apex Predator . . . 28

More Gator Facts . . . 30

Glossary . . . 30

To Learn More . . . 31

Seven Words about an Alligator

Silently floating,

Silently gloating,

Not a log.

The alligator's name comes from Spanish explorers in the 1500s. They had never seen an alligator until they came to the Americas. They called the creature *el lagarto*, which means "the lizard." Some time later, English settlers in the Americas misheard the Spanish term, and the word became *alligator*.

The Alligator's Smile

Do not trust a smiling gator.

She is thinking: *Now? Or later?*

She is plotting how to catch you

In

    a

        while.

When she's done with cogitating

(I'm so sorry to be stating),

She will have an even greater

Mile-

    wide

        smile.

Due to an alligator's snout and jaw structure, its top row of teeth shows even with its mouth closed. So in fact, its smiling appearance has nothing to do with either happiness or a dream of a successful hunt.

Alligator to Himself

Mirror, mirror, in the pond,

You show me one of whom I'm fond.

His length is perfect,

And his hide.

He's not too slim

And not too wide.

His pose? Perfection.

Words all fail.

I love you, gator,

Nose to tail.

We've looked this way

For all to see

Since almost . . .

An eternity.

Using fossil records, scientists have proven that closely related ancestors of alligators lived alongside the dinosaurs. Crocodilians, the group of reptiles including alligators and crocodiles, first appeared about eighty million years ago. Their dinosaur cousins died off sixty-five million years ago, but the crocodilians managed to survive.

Mother and Child, Alligator Style

We think of a mother.

We think of her child.

We think of her loving

And caring and mild.

Most reptile moms, though,

Lay eggs, then move on.

Before those eggs hatch,

That mother is gone.

But not Mama gator.

She watches the nest,

Takes care of her hatchlings.

That's what she does best.

She fights off the snakes,

Otters, bobcats, and bass

Who like to grab gator tots

From the swamp grass.

So watch out, you predators.

Leave them alone,

Or Mama will eat *you*

Right down to the bone.

After mating, the female alligator builds a nest, which may be as large as 10 feet (3 meters) around and 3 feet (0.9 m) high. Then the mother lays her eggs—up to ninety of them! She watches the nest for sixty-five days as the eggs incubate.

When the babies hatch, the mama gator will keep a close eye on them, to protect them from predators—including larger alligators.

Kindergarten for Alligators

First day, learn to prey.

Second day, the same.

Third day, another hunt—

It's our favorite game.

We don't wait for Mother

To help us with our needs.

We swim into the water,

And we learn to read . . .

            the reeds.

A newborn alligator is called a hatchling. Mama gator will help the babies by removing nest debris and making a path for them to the water. As soon as a baby gator gets into the water, it can swim, hide, catch food, and bite. Young alligators eat small fish, insects, snails, mice, worms, frogs, and even other baby alligators!

Sunning

You think that gator's dozing
In the dreamy afternoon.
You're wrong if you're supposing
That he's having a sweet swoon.

He's probably just chilly.
He can't raise his body heat—
But with the warming of the sun,
Can lumber to his feet.

Reptiles such as alligators are cold-blooded, unable to create their own body heat. So an alligator basks in the sun to raise its temperature. If the gator gets too cold, it becomes sluggish, which makes hunting for food difficult. So never mistake a sunning alligator for a *sleeping* alligator.

Alligator in Armor

Much like spiked armor

Is his skin.

It's nature's shield

For what's within.

It's strong and aptly

Called a hide,

Disguising well

What lies inside.

The skin covering most of an adult alligator is very tough and covered with dozens of ridges. These bony ridges are called osteoderms. An adult may be gray, dark olive, muddy brown, or almost black in color, and in some light it can even look deep blue. That helps it hide in the water. But the skin on an alligator's belly is light-colored and smooth.

A young American alligator will also have yellow marks across its body that slowly fade as it ages.

So Many Teeth

Three thousand teeth
In just one jaw?
Not any gator
I ever saw.

Not all at once,
But over a life
Of chewing, biting,
Battle, and strife.

Some teeth wear down,
And some teeth break
On sticks or shells
Or very tough steak.

There's many a way
They lose a tooth.
And that, my friends,
Is a gator truth.

An alligator has between seventy-four and eighty teeth in its mouth at a time. As those teeth wear down or fall out, they are replaced by new teeth that grow in. An alligator can go through two thousand to three thousand teeth in a lifetime.

Mother Alligator on the Path

You think gator's paying no mind

As she's dragging that long tail behind,

But you should not compete

With a gator's swift feet,

For on dawdlers she often has dined.

You think that she's softened, she's kind,

That she's left her bad manners behind.

But she's hungry and greedy

And can be quite speedy

Whenever her stomach's inclined.

Alligators in the water are known for their deadly quick movements, propelled by their strong tails. But don't be fooled by those short legs when the gator is on land. Alligators are capable of running at speeds up to 10 or 11 miles (16 to 18 kilometers) per hour—but only for about 8 yards (7.3 m).

Ambush

The alligator underwater

In the swamp or bog

Quite often seems a harmless rock

Or piece of floating log.

She hides her back, her legs, her tail.

But do not be mistaken.

For if *you* think she's just a log,

You surely will be taken.

Her eager eyes spy out the meal

That swims on unaware,

Then grabs and rolls it in the swamp—

The perfect gator snare.

Alligators are ambush predators. That means they lie hidden until their prey swims by or approaches the water's edge on land. Water, duckweed, and pond scum are excellent camouflage for gators. In this way, they find food without wasting energy on a long chase.

What an Alligator Eats

The question is not what a gator *can* eat.

The question is what she cannot.

We know she devours birds, turtles, and fish,

And eats all those things quite a lot.

She'll grab a raccoon that comes close for a drink.

She will eat snakes and ducks and crustaceans.

She'll devour a creature that's small or quite big.

She waits for her food with great patience.

The stomachs of gators, when opened, have shown

That gators eat anything near:

Golf balls as well as a parcel of plums,

Golf shoes as well as a deer.

So, when walking your dog near the bayou, beware.

Be ready to run, and don't fall.

For a gator that's hungry may scurry and snap,

And grab your poor pooch, leash and all.

Once alligators mature, they eat mainly fish, turtles, and waterbirds. They also kill animals such as muskrats, otters, and raccoons that come down to the water's edge to drink. Larger, more powerful gators can even take down deer, antelope, and cows.

Obituary

Alligators live long lives.

They don't seem to grow old.

They just get bigger, longer.

They remain both fast and bold.

Without a sign of their old age,

They pace the swampy shore

For up to half a century—

Zoo gators even more.

Scientists think alligators in the wild can live for up to fifty years. Some gators in zoos have lived more than seventy years. The oldest captive gator is in the Belgrade Zoo, in Serbia. Muja arrived at that zoo in 1937, fully grown—probably at least ten years old already. How old do you think he might be?

Apex Predator

The gator outlived the dinosaur,

At eighty million years or more,

Which may have seemed like a distinction

Till the threat of mass extinction

Threatened—

'Cause it's true

That the famous apex predators

(So deemed by science editors)

Were slowly being apexed out

By

YOU.

Crocodilians have been some of the world's top predators since the dinosaurs died out. But during the 1900s, humans almost killed off American alligators. People used their skins for luggage and clothing and ate alligator meat. They ruined alligator habitats by draining swamps for agriculture and golf courses.

The American alligator was named an endangered species in 1967. The US government limited alligator hunting and set up protected habitat areas. Twenty years later, gators moved off the endangered species list because the population had recovered so well.

More Gator Facts

- An average adult female American alligator is 8.2 feet (2.5 m) long and weighs about 200 pounds (91 kilograms). Males are larger, averaging 11.2 feet (3.4 m) long and up to 500 pounds (227 kg). Big males can actually be more than 20 feet (6.1 m) long, snout to tail. That's longer than a full-size pickup truck!

- Alligators have nostrils that face upward. So a gator can keep most of its body under water, with just its snout and nostrils peeking out, and breathe air from above. Its eyes also have an extra eyelid that covers the eye whenever the alligator submerges. It's like having built-in goggles.

- American alligators can be found in the southeastern United States. Louisiana has the largest population, with about two million gators. They also live in Florida, Mississippi, Georgia, Alabama, North Carolina, South Carolina, Oklahoma, Arkansas, and Texas. Another species of alligator lives in China.

- Although gators do hunt onshore, they snag most of their meals under water. For a recent study, scientists strapped cameras to fifteen different American alligators in coastal Florida. The videos showed that underwater ambushes were twice as successful as when the gator hunted at the water's surface.

Glossary

apex predator: top predator in a particular food chain

bask: to lie in the warmth of the sun

bayou: a marshy outlet of a lake or river in the American South

cogitating: thinking deeply about

crustaceans: a group of animals with a hard outer shell, including shrimp, lobster, and crabs

dawdler: someone who moves extremely slow

osteoderm: a bony deposit or plate found in the skin

predator: an animal that hunts other animals for food

prey: an animal that is hunted and killed for food

To Learn More

American Alligator Fact Sheet–National Zoo
http://nationalzoo.si.edu/Animals/ReptilesAmphibians/Facts/FactSheets/Americanalligator.cfm
What are alligators fed at the National Zoo in Washington, DC? Visit this page for that answer and lots more interesting facts!

American Alligators–*National Geographic*
http://animals.nationalgeographic.com/animals/reptiles/american-alligator/
Check out a map of where American alligators live, and listen to a sound clip of an alligator.

A Guide to Living with Alligators
http://myfwc.com/media/152524/Alligator_Brochure.pdf
Learn more about how alligators and people can safely share home territory in this online brochure from the Florida Fish and Wildlife Conservation Commission.

Heos, Bridget. *What to Expect When You're Expecting Hatchlings*. Minneapolis: Millbrook Press, 2012.
Discover key facts about alligators, crocodiles, caimans, and their hatchlings in this humorous guide.

Rockwell, Anne. *Who Lives in an Alligator Hole?* New York: Collins, 2006.
Alligators are a vital part of their home areas. Find out what makes these hunters a "keystone species"–the most important animal in their habitat.

Silverman, Buffy. *Can You Tell an Alligator from a Crocodile?* Minneapolis: Lerner Publications, 2012.
Through clear photos and fascinating facts, become an expert on telling these look-alikes apart.

About the Author and Photographer

Jane Yolen is the author of more than 350 books, many of which are about natural science including *Owl Moon, Bird Watch*, and *A Ring of Seasons*, plus fourteen books of poetry and science with her award-winning photographer son, Jason Stemple.

Jason Stemple, whose books have won both the John Burroughs Nature Books for Young Readers Award and the National Outdoor Book Award, has been a photographer since his college days. He received a 2011 Everglades Fellowship to shoot there for a month, with trail access and a cabin for his use. A number of the alligators featured in this book are from that trip, and the rest are from near his home in Charleston, South Carolina.